For: *Joyce*

From: *Kay*

1995

Celebrating
Nature

Heartland Samplers, Inc.
Edina, Minnesota
Printed in Hong Kong.

Celebrating Nature
Copyright © 1992, Heartland Samplers, Inc.
5555 W 78th St., Suite P
Edina, MN 55439

Original artwork by Kit Shoop

Product #707
ISBN 0-944884-42-3

Celebrating

Nature

"My name is Margalo,"
said the bird, softly, in a
small voice. "I come from
fields once tall with wheat,
from pastures deep in fern
and thistle; I come from
vales of meadowsweet, and
I love to whistle."

E.B. White

Autumn was kind to them,
the winter was long to them
— but in April, late April,
all the gold sang. Spring
came that year like magic
and like song. One day its
breath was in the air....

Thomas Wolfe

When I look at the sky, which you have made, at the moon and the stars, which you set in their places — what is man that you think of him....

Psalm 8

In the beginning God created heaven and earth ...and God saw everything that he had made, and it was very good.

Psalm 1

The very act of planting a
seed in the earth has in it to
me something beautiful. I
always do it with a joy that
is largely mixed with awe.
Celia Thaxter

I watch my garden beds after they are sown, and think how one of God's exquisite miracles is going on beneath the dark earth out of sight. I never forget my planted seeds.

Celia Thaxter

Yes, the sowing of a seed seems a very simple matter, but I always feel as if it were a sacred thing among the mysteries of God.

Celia Thaxter

And now these three
remain: faith, hope and
love. But the greatest of
these is love.

1 Corinthians 13:13

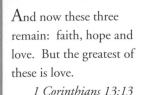

And those who are peacemakers will plant seeds of peace and reap a harvest of goodness.

James 3:18

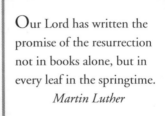

Our Lord has written the promise of the resurrection not in books alone, but in every leaf in the springtime.

Martin Luther

The tiniest dewdrop hanging from a grass blade in the morning is big enough to reflect the sunshine and the blue of the sky.

I like to think of nature as an unlimited radio station, through which God speaks to us every hour, if we will only tune in.

George Washington Carver

The amen of Nature is always a flower.

Oliver Wendell Holmes

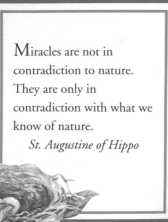

Miracles are not in contradiction to nature. They are only in contradiction with what we know of nature.

St. Augustine of Hippo

It was so beautiful — the dewy quiet, the freshness, the long, still shadows, the matchless, delicate, sweet charm of the newly wakened world.

Celia Thaxter

The earth is the Lord's, and the fulness thereof; the world, and they that dwell therein.

Psalm 24

If I keep a green bough in my heart, the singing bird will come.

For mine is just a little old-fashioned garden where the flowers come together to praise the Lord and teach all who look upon them to do likewise.

Celia Thaxter

No one really knows a
bird until he has seen it
in flight.

Henry Beston

A pleasure shared is a pleasure doubled. I always like to have companions on my tramps through the woods.

John Kieran

My father still goes out every spring, and he's now eighty, and plants an apple tree. Next year he plans on starting oaks...now that's really faith!

Were there no God, we would be in this glorious world with grateful hearts and no one to thank.

Christina Rossetti

The flowers appear on the earth; the time of the singing of birds is come, and the voice of the turtle dove is heard in our land.

Song of Solomon

Earth's crammed with heaven.

Elizabeth Barrett Browning

Like the tide...some things...arrive in their own mysterious hour, on their own terms and not yours, to be seized or relinquished forever.

Godwin

We often take for granted
the very things that most
deserve our gratitude.

Ozick

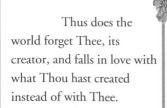

Thus does the world forget Thee, its creator, and falls in love with what Thou hast created instead of with Thee.

St. Augustine of Hippo

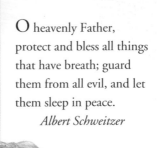

O heavenly Father,
protect and bless all things
that have breath; guard
them from all evil, and let
them sleep in peace.

Albert Schweitzer

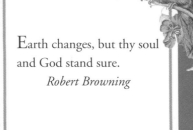

Earth changes, but thy soul
and God stand sure.

Robert Browning

These beautiful days must enrich all my life. They saturate themselves into every part of the body and live always.

T. H. Watkins

The sky is the daily bread
of the eyes.
Ralph Waldo Emerson

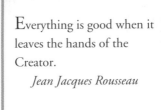

Everything is good when it leaves the hands of the Creator.

Jean Jacques Rousseau

God writes the Gospel not in the Bible alone, but on trees, and flowers, and clouds, and stars.

Martin Luther King

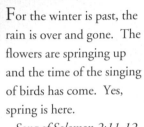

For the winter is past, the rain is over and gone. The flowers are springing up and the time of the singing of birds has come. Yes, spring is here.

Song of Solomon 2:11-12

It is possible to be still enough to enjoy companionship with God.

J. Gustav White

Thy Word is like a garden, Lord,
With flowers bright and fair;
And every one who seeks
May pluck a lovely cluster there.

Edwin Hodder

What nature-lover's
tongue can tell,
What golden pen portray
The outpoured, flaming
splendors
Of a bright September day?

Charles G. Stater

The morning stars still sing together, and the world, not yet half made, becomes more beautiful every day.

Dewitt Jones

We need wilderness
whether or not we ever set
foot in it. We need a
refuge even though we may
never need to go there.
Edward Abbey

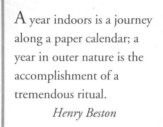

A year indoors is a journey
along a paper calendar; a
year in outer nature is the
accomplishment of a
tremendous ritual.

Henry Beston

There are many pleasing sounds in nature. The sound of the canyon wren, tripping down, down, down the scale, fills one with lightsomeness.

The Voice of the Coyote

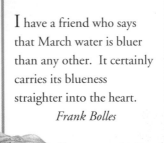

I have a friend who says
that March water is bluer
than any other. It certainly
carries its blueness
straighter into the heart.
Frank Bolles

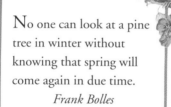

No one can look at a pine tree in winter without knowing that spring will come again in due time.

Frank Bolles

I do not know when it was, nor where it was, nor how young I may have been, but I can recall...a sudden feeling of happiness at hearing the voice of the pines.

Frank Bolles

If we are in tune with Nature, all her music can find a way into the heart. When bird music is rare, their occasional songs are precious to the ear.

Frank Bolles

Spring came that year like magic and like music and like song. One day its breath was in the air.

Thomas Wolfe

There is no creature, regardless of its apparent insignificance, that fails to show us something of God's goodness.

Thomas À Kempis

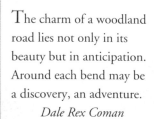

The charm of a woodland
road lies not only in its
beauty but in anticipation.
Around each bend may be
a discovery, an adventure.
Dale Rex Coman

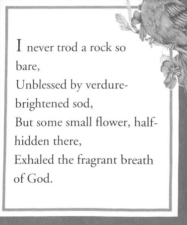

I never trod a rock so bare,
Unblessed by verdure-brightened sod,
But some small flower, half-hidden there,
Exhaled the fragrant breath of God.

The little cares that
fretted me,
I lost them yesterday,
Among the fields above
the sea,
Among the winds at play.

This is my Father's world — His own design, but in His goodness He has made it mine!

Faye Carr Adams

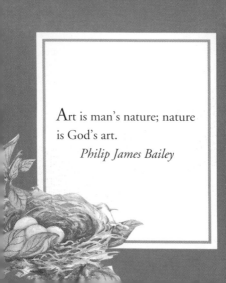

Art is man's nature; nature is God's art.

Philip James Bailey

"Look at us," said the violets blooming at her feet. "All last winter we slept in seeming death, but at the right time God awakened us, and here we are to comfort you."

Edward Payson Rod

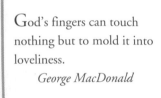

God's fingers can touch
nothing but to mold it into
loveliness.

George MacDonald

Father, thank You that
You took time to create
beauty; how can I be too
busy to appreciate it?
Amen.

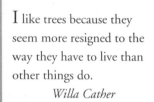

I like trees because they seem more resigned to the way they have to live than other things do.

Willa Cather

When in these fresh mornings I go into my garden before any one is awake, I go for the time being into perfect happiness.

Celia Thaxter

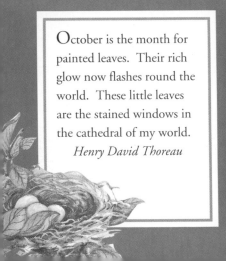

October is the month for painted leaves. Their rich glow now flashes round the world. These little leaves are the stained windows in the cathedral of my world.

Henry David Thoreau

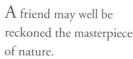

A friend may well be
reckoned the masterpiece
of nature.
Ralph Waldo Emerson

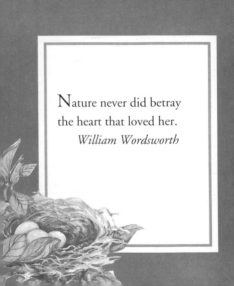

Nature never did betray
the heart that loved her.
William Wordsworth

"You never saw anything so beautiful! It has come!
I thought it had come that other morning, but it was
only coming. It is here now! It has come, the
Spring!"

Frances Hodgson Burnett

The woods would be very silent if no birds sang there except those who sang best.

Audubon

No man is an island,
entire of itself; every man is
a piece of the continent, a
part of the main.

John Donne

Slow buds the pink dawn
like a rose
From out night's gray
and cloudy sheath;
Softly and still it grows
and grows,
Petal by petal, leaf by leaf.
Susan Coolidge

There is nothing more eloquent in Nature than a mountain stream.

John Muir

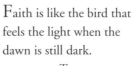

Faith is like the bird that
feels the light when the
dawn is still dark.

Tagore

Joys come from simple and natural things: mists over meadows, sunlight on leaves, the path of the moon over water.

Sigurd F. Olson

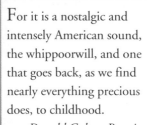

For it is a nostalgic and intensely American sound, the whippoorwill, and one that goes back, as we find nearly everything precious does, to childhood.

Donald Culross Peattie

I am not...certain that I want to be able to identify all the warblers. There is a charm sometimes in not knowing what or who the singer is.

Donald Culross Peattie

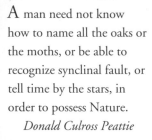

A man need not know
how to name all the oaks or
the moths, or be able to
recognize synclinal fault, or
tell time by the stars, in
order to possess Nature.

Donald Culross Peattie

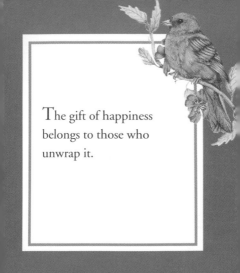

The gift of happiness
belongs to those who
unwrap it.

Instead of a gem or even a flower, cast the gift of a lovely thought into the heart of a friend.

Happiness held is the seed;
happiness shared is the
flower.

By nature all men are much alike, but by education they become different.

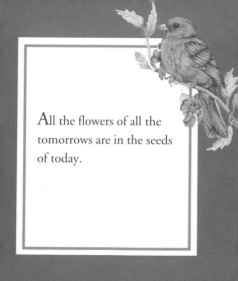

All the flowers of all the tomorrows are in the seeds of today.

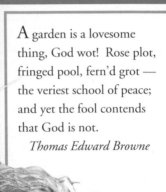

A garden is a lovesome thing, God wot! Rose plot, fringed pool, fern'd grot — the veriest school of peace; and yet the fool contends that God is not.

Thomas Edward Browne

I have been thinking about the change of seasons. I don't want to miss spring this year. I want to be there on the spot the moment the grass turns green.

Pilgrim at Tinker Creek

It is only a little planet
But how beautiful it is.

Robert Jeffers

One moment of a man's life is a fact so stupendous as to take the lustre out of all fiction.

Ralph Waldo Emerson

You're only here for a short visit. Don't hurry, don't worry, and stop to smell the flowers along the way.

It is my experience that, when a nightingale starts singing, the small birds near immediately become attentive, often suspending their own songs. And some fly to perch near him and listen.

William Henry Hudson

The hours when the mind is absorbed by beauty are the only hours when we really live.

Richard Jefferies

I am a boy again
sitting in a meadow at
twilight with my farmer
friend, the filly grazing
nearby, and the
Whippoorwill is calling to
me out of the midst of
vanished years.

John Kieran

To care for the living earth
is to care for ourselves.

If indeed thy heart were right, then would every creature be to thee a mirror of life, and a book of holy doctrine.

Thomas À Kempis

The setting sun will always set me aright...if a sparrow comes before my window, I take part in his existence and pick about in the gravel.

John Keats

Like winds and sunsets,
wild things were taken for
granted until progress
began to do away with
them.

Aldo Leopold

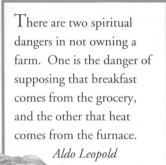

There are two spiritual
dangers in not owning a
farm. One is the danger of
supposing that breakfast
comes from the grocery,
and the other that heat
comes from the furnace.

Aldo Leopold

Thus came the lovely spring, with a rush of blossoms and music, flooding the earth with flowers.

Henry Wadsworth Longfellow

Nature is painting for us, day after day, pictures of infinite beauty if only we have the eyes to see them.

John Ruskin

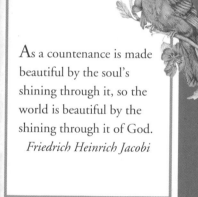

As a countenance is made beautiful by the soul's shining through it, so the world is beautiful by the shining through it of God.

Friedrich Heinrich Jacobi

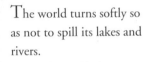

The world turns softly so as not to spill its lakes and rivers.

Conkling

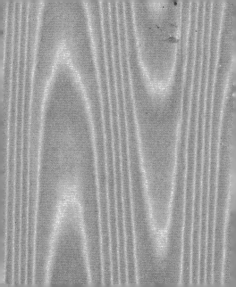